# Year 2 Poet

Year 2 Poet

Copyright ©2015 by Lori Kane

Cover by: Bridget Beorse

ISBN-13: 978-0-9862996-6-7
ISBN-10: 0-9862996-6-9

Lori Kane
www.collectiveself.com
Email: lori@collectiveself.com

Share feedback on the book at:
feedback@collectiveself.com

Printed by Createspace. An Amazon.com company.

# Year 2 Poet

by

Lori Kane

For Daniel

# Contents

# Year 2 Poet

# Prologue

If you read Year 1 Poet, you'll know that being a first-year poet was rough. Wonder-filled, yes, and yet hard because of my constant self-doubt and worry.

My first year as a poet played out as follows:

1. Exhausted by 21 years in the city, I moved to an island.

2. I spent the first four months on the island totally freaking out, because I could only write poetry, not essays anymore. Which felt really weird at the time.

3. I spent another four months feeling lost because I had no idea what I was doing writing poetry, or why, but I kept doing it anyway. I suspect it was mostly because new neighbors — who'd read my blog — showed up and called me a poet. That was pretty cool.

4. I spent the last four months of the year admitting to myself that I enjoy being lost, most days, and that I adore being a poet. And then creating the book Year 1 Poet, which I imagined was the first book in a 5-year series about both the experience of becoming a poet and the poetry itself.

5. Across that year, I remembered that I'd written poetry as a kid — from grade school through high school — something that 25 years of adulthood had almost erased from my memory. In Year 1, I re-found artist me and I resurrected her. The sections of the book Year 1 Poet reflected what it took to remember myself as an artist: slowing down, loving more deeply, allowing myself to play more, exploring identity (What Does a Poet Do?), and receiving support. That was Year 1.

Being a second-year poet was considerably different.

It was a bit easier as a poet: I wasn't completely freaking out. Yet it was much harder as a human: my extended family shattered after my grandmother passed away.

I listened and watched in horror as many of my revered elders began acting like scared and wounded children. Turning on each other. Blaming each other. Sides were formed. A judge and lawyers were involved. Horrible, unforgivable things were said by people I love to other people I love. Some relationships shattered. It felt like my heart and limbs were being ripped from my body some days. I found myself living the day that I now realize all of us must live at some point: the day you realize that you yourself must become (or have already become) a family elder. What a horrible, horrible day that is.

In Year 2, it was my artist self who saved me, not the other way around.

She visibly stayed with pain, accepting and allowing pain to become fully part of us: teaching me how to sit still in the heart of fire and look around. How to eventually move as pain, with pain, instead of ignoring it, hiding from it, squirrelling it away and allowing it to pool and stagnate into contempt and bitterness and resentment within me.

She visibly moved with reverence: surfacing the lovely and holy ordinary. She gifted poetry to others every chance she got and was with me when I noticed that the poetry that I'd created and given to others was often gifted back to me the moment I needed it.

She prioritized creation: spending more time with other poets and writers and painters and musicians and artists, and their work. She demanded time to write no matter how busy or bad things got. This meant that finally, at 44, I myself regularly made it onto my own Top 10 Priorities list this year.

And she followed her own curiosity down rabbit holes into wondrous places, reminding me that there are countless worlds to explore and universes to stumble upon. Making me feel like a kid again.

This, friends, is Year 2.

# 1. Moving in Reverence

# Beside the House of Worship

By the sea
on the sidewalk of my own neighborhood
grass-brown rabbits startle, dart away
on my walks I see more back feet
more flashes of tail
than peep-show patrons on pay day

Beside the wet sidewalk
in town near the center for the arts
after we poets convene
three fat black rabbits picnic
a fourth fellow yawns
a fifth bathes conspicuously, back foot on high

I startle, look away
that was close, too much presence
more of God than I expected
I dart away home

my pastor is poetry
my imam imagination
my rabbis are rabbits

wow
even poet gatherings
flashes of heaven: my nuns on Sunday
can't compare

come silence
come sweet true self
take patience by the hand
meet us outside in the tall grass
beside the house of worship

# Hearth Fire

Mom
I love the way you love
warm folding of laundry
soft fuzzy robes
drying dishes, the game of where
to put them
you rubbing my hands and feet
always present for me
here beyond memory

so let synapses misfire
let brains tinder the fire of smiling hearts

I thought Alzheimer's was a fire burning away at us
until a predilection to leave the essential untouched
became infinitely obvious
burning away instead the noisy distance
that too-busy charade
our frustration, guilt, shame, regret, fear, anger, contempt
even sorrow
mine yours ours
until they fade into background:
dust bunnies, ember elves
shadow puppets
former selves

I was so then
so blind
Alzheimer's is not a flame to burn us

We are the flame

we release demons
set them in boats
kick their sterns and cut their ropes
we set then adrift
here in the now
you become hearth fire
I become sky
at ease within all dis-ease
just us again
like always
giggling above the laundry

# Almost Imperceptibly Earth

opens
when we welcome

shifts
when we dance

riffs
when we improv

crinkles
when we laugh

slows
when we listen

aches
when we weep

changes
when we change

rocks us
to sleep

# I Break My Heart Each Morning

I break my heart each morning
so there is room for her

her memory and story
her history inside of me

disease that slowly separates
her away from her

beyond disease
a slow release
of precious self to daughters

Mom
we break ourselves each morning
let our hearts be wounds
now find those hearts
a gentle gauze
wound around the world

# Beauty Does Not Stay Down

before you mourn your mom smiling out from behind the gauze
of her disease, remember

        beauty will not sit down

before you expect your dad to be reasonable, to let go of both
Mom, and who he is, this instant, remember

        beauty will not sit down

before you ask your cousin, yourself, to abandon rage about grief
and loss, remember

        beauty will not sit down

before you say goodbye to someone, certain your story ends here,
remember

        beauty will not sit down

before you expect someone to stop being so negative all the time,
remember

        beauty will not sit down

before you apologize for being yourself again, remember

        beauty will not sit down

before you concern yourself with their motives, with yours,
remember

        beauty will not sit down

before you feel wounded by words spoken at the table, or online
words pouring forth from countless lifetimes of brethren in streets
gunned down, remember Mike Brown

        beauty will not sit down

before you look away in horror from girls bought and sold for sex
and pennies, recall

     beauty will not stay down

before you accept what is said about you, about us, as the truth,
remember

     beauty will not stay down

before you decide you're not brave enough for this life
curl up, rest, recall
the seed in the ground

      you will rise up again

      you will rise again

      you rise again

      you rise

      you

      !


     beauty does not stay down

# Content to Be Everything

lit from above
warming green leaves with dusted-red edges
unfurl new
learning of selves connected

I am leaf branch tree
runner root seed
forest perch
food and shelter
paper pencil book
board house home

earth-bound at times
floating free at times
wind-bent sometimes
rain-fed sometimes
at times felled
at times drowned

destroyed and reimagined often

yet content

as everything content

content to be everything

# Becoming Magic With Her

I love Alzheimer's

when Mom looks into my eyes
says "My baby girl. I love you."
twinkles
hugs me close
she lifts the world to my lips
pours gratitude through me

inconsequential then
that names are dead
past is gone
old us drowned

we float happy here

no longer up to us to judge selves
fix others
worry needlessly
fret about what we don't have
who we aren't
carry world weight
harbor regret

we are free together
entirely
every moment I let us be

so I let us be

becoming magic with her

# Talking with Neighbors

I was telling my neighbor how much I appreciate the multigenerational knowledge and friendship in our new (to us) neighborhood: a rare gift — at least in my world — people holding on to a 6-generation understanding of a place. He said he appreciated it too and also loves that he got to be alive in the 1960s: the last decade that our country had fully functional small towns where everybody made something, fixed something, shared something, and we weren't dependent on big distant corporations and Dairy Queen back then.

My neighbor said that at his age he's come to value the tribe here. What our political differences happen to be, matter far less now. What *any* of our divisive differences are matter far less now. You become more curious, he said: What is this tribe here about? And what am I in this tribe? When you're my age, he said.

And my age, I thought, perhaps presumptuously, given that I wasn't alive in the 1960s.

I mentioned that my parents just picked a town because it's close to us, though thousands of miles from their heritage home. Plus there are three credit unions to choose from, which makes bank-hating Dad happy, and a Subway sandwich shop, which makes Mom, who has Alzheimer's disease, happy. There she still knows the menu, ingredients, and the process plus she loves their raspberry white chocolate chip cookies. It's one of the few restaurants left on earth in which she can relax and enjoy life. The neighborhood they picked has independent living cottages + assisted living + memory care: the trifecta of awesomeness from their new perspective, that *and* there's a Walmart just down the hill from their new place so they can easily do one-stop shopping and pick up their prescriptions.

Lately I've been dropping the need to be sad or worried or mad about Mom and Dad's very different selves and priorities now. Together we're fine most days. Beyond fine. I've also been dropping my own need to hate Subway and Walmart: not that I'm typically a patron of either when Mom and Dad aren't around (my ridiculous ego would deeply like you to know).

Frankly, I'm in awe at the glorious simplicity of their lives now.

Where:

> small loving family + supportive neighborhood
> + nearby credit union + Subway + Walmart
> = pure contentment and peace

And I've been shifting into the growing simplicity of my own life.

Where:

> the universe giggles while a progressive, Walmart-hating daughter
> openly admits Walmart's place
> in her own beloved parent's current happiness.

The world is not as simple as we would like it to be.

Then again,
it is simple here walking
talking with neighbors.

# 2. Staying with Pain

# Winter's Orphans Springtime's Clowns

## I.

with tears,
cloaked in half-truths
clinging to vague, unexamined fear and rage
the adults turned
scattered to earth's farthest corners
from great distance
built walls
weapons
did battle.

Fucking grownups.

## II.

Left behind on wide open plains
Winter's abandoned children faced hard choices
no choice, really

stay
face
more-whole truths
broken hearts everywhere
loss
anger on all sides
fear everywhere
the worst within

hold on
to fun
laughter

honor
lightness of spirit
darkness of origin

create
impossible new old selves
disinclined to hide

glide down, through, then off of hatred
hands up in the air
like a slide

sit with the
weeping
stay with abandoned
selves
cry with the
wounded
cradle the
dying
embrace the
dead

accept the cracks

accept abandonment

accept the rage that moves through you

accept this new state of orphanhood, this too-soon adulthood
like you watched your cousins do
once before
rising from ashes
more amazing than ever
beautiful, wise, kinder, gentler, made strong
on winter's harsh plane

### III.

With grownups fled
your first instincts were to rush to fix things,
build walls out of hatred, and/or run away.
To look away, sequester yourself, like the adults did.

But utterly surrounded by orphans,
new options arrived
new voices
the trees, the stars, all the dead
whisper

Not yet child. Be still.
First relax, be held.
Be held by your own arms: now your own mother/father.
Be held by the family that remains:
mother universe, father time, mother nature, other orphans.
Stay with it. Name it. Don't rush.
Grieve. Rage. Mourn. Collapse.
Give in to the urge to play when you're ready.
Play as if Life herself depended on it.
Be amazed: they are enough
More amazed: you are enough

gather internal strength this winter
look deeper
until you find slivers of uncertainty within certainty
greater truths around untruths
seeds for doing better:
vulnerability
lightly held connection
shared pain
humor
a secret love of winter, even as we curse it, shovel it
friendship

jump up and down in anger
until you remember, feel
the pure joy in jumping
up
and down

notice
how you yourself moved your anger through you
in through your head
out your now-warm feet

## IV.

with almost invisible seeds
they themselves can't clearly see
Winter's badass children will rebuild themselves
until they're laughing
until we're all laughing
who better to start a sacred choir of laughter
than Winter's abandoned children
united as friends
content with who they are
held within loss
jumping up and down
kickstarting lost humanity
powered from within?

## V.

we are Winter's badass orphans

abandoned
we break
rage
mourn
play
start over
with broken, lost selves
raw
bare and unhidden
vulnerable
yet remarkably held

Adults may never understand our silly.
They forgot the power of silly.

yet couldn't fully pull content from within discontent
or find mystery and wonder within ruin
without it

Bitches, we can.

We can Scooby Fucking Doo this.

## VI.

walls we once cursed, like our parents,
we taught ourselves to cherish
those walls meant becoming our own elders
forming more open, silly, bleeding hearts within ourselves
broken hearts, perfect, for turning walls into playgrounds

the same walls that made enemies
of our too distant parents
are making
better parents
better community members
better leaders
crafters, builders, farmers
artists, poets
and elders
right now
of us all

watch us demonstrate

## VII.

Dear, dear, fucking grownups
Good God it's hard to love you some days

but we do
we love you
we honor you
by making different choices than you did

happy humans don't appear magically come springtime
not yet they don't
peace for us means slowing down together
crafting new selves
from raw red earth, rubble, spit, and bubble gum
right now

we know we need every unique perspective
every person
to survive, thrive

You forgot that your own children are abandoned
behind your walls.
Orphaning you within.

Welcome to our world, orphan.
Running away is not an option here.
Walls and distance and distraction don't work here.
Here we face the music together, awkwardly re-learn to dance,
or we die trying.

The empty world you left us is cold, shattered.
Walls in all directions we turn.
Can't you hear us screaming outside your fortresses?
Open your eyes. We're not monsters, dear hearts.
We're all just abandoned children.
We will see this for you if you can't
through your self-blinded eyes.

## VIII.

We pulled ourselves through the harshest winter
together
hand in hand
with those we love

those you failed to teach us to hate

we have become our own elders

your generation will be the last to die
trying to heal across great distances
behind walls, blind,
stuck, drowning in smelly, stagnant rage

ours will be the last one abandoned
to die alone in the street

this shit stops with us

## IX.

our children
will watch us work with neighbors
to tear down old walls
build parks

our children
will help us plant vegetables
in abandoned lots
fruit on rooftops
herbs in pots

our children
will hear us creating art, laughing
with those we were taught to hate

our children
will grow up laughing and crying together
unafraid
to bring their fears out in the open
in rubble-magic playgrounds
emerging as springtime's clowns.

Until this rings true for all our children
this rings hollow for all our children.

This is our truth. We own it. We don't look away.
We are offering our lives — Gens X, Y, Z — to bring this
through.

## X.

Welcome the clowns.

Weaving wounds together
with
love and humor
stayed-with grief
MOAR gratitude!

soft twinkles in their eyes
gentle curious flexible fingers and souls
finding and using wordless threads —
goose bumps, belly laughs, cheek-tears, skipping, pee-inducing
giggles, and awe —
pulling wounded worlds back together

bowing deeper silly bows

mourning wide open, visible and exposed

allowing the dead

finally honored

to go.

# Our Fevered State

## 1. Pain and Shock

I lay in bed this week
fevered and in pain
energy drained
throat on fire
tired and sick

while screens around me
surface a young white face
with stone dead eye sockets
murderer, 9 times over
lily white terrorist
with a Dorothy Hamill haircut
imagined into killer
wounder of our heart, lovely Charleston

from bed
in my fevered state
I see a zombie
Am I alone in this?
the walking dead
those eyes
God, those eyes
night of the living dead

## 2. Facing It

Home Grown Delusion

My People Are Terrorists

These are my headlines.
I write them crying.
Won't move past them alone.

I called myself sick before but I'm not sick.
I am ill: unwell for now.
I'm drinking juice, resting, sniffling, reflecting
talking with friends and family here and afar
creating something new
I will recover: alive and beyond lucky.

Sick — I notice in his eyes through my tears—is something else.

Sick is stuck.
Unable to move through delusion to see clearly again.
Unable to show up and allow yourself to become
something new together.
Sick allows fear to take you so completely
that your eyes become stones in sockets.
Ears can't recognize the voice of humanity.

Sick is a community state. A sludge individuals get stuck in.
Community vomit.

A white community
white words, websites
draped in sludge
locked in terror of the other
separated from wider reality
lacking access to more alive humanity
they misplace their own souls

We, not they, Lori.

We have so much sludge here.
Into it we sacrifice too many gentle white boys
raising zombies from pools of vomit instead:
bringers of horror and death

Sick political community, media community,
corporate community:
pouring forth zombie pundits
reporters
politicians

zombie captains of industry believing
humans have no innate right to water (Google it)
"leaders"
wind-up dolls with fake spray-on expressions
pretending at grownup-ness
succeeding only at meanness
Imagining evil with unlaughing faces and unweeping eyes

Not facing their own truths. Let alone Our truths.

Autopilot Words
Doctrine Zombies
Blind Flag Wavers in the face of suffering

These are my people. My people.

This is me. Good God.

3. Three Deep Breaths

## 4. An Acceptance Prayer

This is us. This is me.

blind flawed clueless biased still learning

Good God, whatever I am
however blind flawed clueless biased and still learning I am
please God don't let that be me.

Let me not be a zombie.
Let me not be on autopilot.
Let me not separate the suffering of others from my own.
Let me put no symbol, fabric flag, beloved idea, heritage,
book, or property
above tender, living breathing beings.
Let me not be a terrorist.
Let me simply value the living and the breathing and
the being here together.
Let me allow my judgments to be a step backward into my soul
on the way to greater insight.
Let me then trust the words that bubble up within me:
allowing them to wait to come forth, when they want to, and to
spill forth hard and fast when they must.
Let me stay soft and weeping and human,
even in my hardest moments.

While I am breathing, let me never stop crying and laughing.

## 5. The Enough Moment

I just sat outside on the ground for an hour by myself.
The ground is healing, have you noticed?

It's no wonder why people want no part of our big old systems.
Not nearly enough sitting on the earth.
Sick systems. Stuck on repeat. Trapped in delusion.
Human hearts ache for more.
Instead of admitting that we don't know what to do,
asking for help, forgiveness,

or even just stopping and resting and reflecting,
we keep pumping out zombies.

Enough

Sit on the earth. Feel it. Breathe it.
This is the world. Soft breezes, rain, sunshine. My world. Us.
This.

I have had enough of the zombie machine.

Enough

## 6. The Words of a Living Being in the USA

The idea that handguns be required in sacred space is untenable.
Beyond nonsense. Delusional leaps to mind.

Not you. Not wonderful, lovely you.

The idea.

I see that the idea makes sense to those standing in hell.

But I am so very weary of joining you in hell.

I am so weary of dead children and pastors and mothers and
brothers.
So weary of blame.

Would you consider joining me here on the earth?

Just for a minute?

I propose that we allow handguns and automatic weapons
to be required of us only in unsacred space: aka, hell

This is earth. We are hers.
She is beautiful and life giving and, yes, scarily unpredictable.

But this is not hell.

I am so sorry for your pain. I feel it. Weep with you.

And I can no longer imagine earth into hell with you.

I am done allowing myself to take any part in reimagining her into hell.

I am woman.

I am earth.

This is our home. This is us.

We can imagine better together.

It's time to live a new story about our full power.

## 7. A Farewell to the Old Me

Self,
if you are saying the same thing right now that you always say,
hearing what you always hear, I'm sorry,
that is not quite wellness or growth or wholeness or love
or healing
that is not quite living, and worse
That is not you.

You are far more creative than that.

You may walk into a space with hatred in your heart
but you breathe more slowly then
listen more deeply then
feel something new, think something new
then let yourself go into new possibility then
awestruck and humbled
you drop the weapon from your human hand
weep, apologize
are embraced, welcomed home
you are fed
Nothing better than potluck and forgiveness.

The potential power of our collective heart is limitless.
That is the power that persists in the black American community
this week: freer of hearts.
And in the LGBT community this week: freer of brighter,
sassier (no, I-won't-stop-dancing-bitches) souls.

An individual heart can be fooled.

An individual mind can be steeped in delusion too:
faster and far longer than collective hearts can be.

What am I doing right now to tap into the collective heart?
Can I feel it beating within us?
Yes, I can.
Goodbye old us, old me.

Thank you for getting us here.

## 8. New Questions

How many more zombie generations am I willing to see us raise?

How many more years am I willing to ask black and LGBT and
Muslim American families to stand weeping
on courthouse steps
being the shining examples of human love, forgiveness,
and generosity
that I myself ought to be?

Can I face all our fears, pain, history, and dreams?
name them? surface them? feel them? hold them?
be held by them?

Can we wake up from old delusions changed, together,
with hearts alive?

Can I allow my mind to be uncertain and open:
completely lost and oddly comforted
to find myself in yet another new place
with even more people who feel like home?

## 9. This is What Being Well Feels Like

rising
stretching
becoming human again
stumbling
uncertainty
sorrow
despair
weeping

being foolish, laughing
mouth-dropping wonder
being held
learning
holding space
pure delight
rising to become human again

Looking out with eyes that weep and shine and get
frustrated and sparkle together, not zombie eyes

Laughing then crying then laughing at ourselves together.

Rag tag. Imperfect.

We look like chaos and we feel like home.

Remembering our past, living our now, is the same thing
always creating
always in mourning
always helping each other
always experimenting and making mistakes
always starting again
together and alone, more certain this time…

### 10. Imagining What Being Even More Well Could Look Like

More rainbows
More people feeling loved, welcome, home

More dreams
Fewer early-death- and walking-dead-bringing
delusions

Crying publicly encouraged

When fallen or failed or exhausted within one community,
individuals move fluidly into others
to find their people, their healing, elsewhere
bravely, like children, musicians, artists, poets
bearing our most precious instruments:
hearts that cannot be fashioned into weapons

A generation of humans saying:
"Mine was the last generation willing to gun ourselves down"

## 11. My Country, Poetry

In my country, poetry
we value creativity
cherish weird and levity
true-to-self natures
diving all in
safe, supporting, silly, sensitive, subversive
— all the best S's

In my country, poetry
we are compass
bad ass
bullshit cutlass
impolite, uncouth
fragile and fiercely open
embracing sorrow and pain publicly
letting go of self repeatedly
wild rose responsible
wild horse free

Here we grow more trusting and trusted with age.
Here we play at being rainbows.
see each other through God's eyes
hold each other with Goddess hands
weep as humans
part as friends

In my country, poetry
monsters are pulled forth around campfires
reminding us of our past, then
taking off our zombie masks
we join the living in a dance
muddy feet soon find the beat

beneath these now more-spacious skies

# Family Drift

### 1. The Question

*Why do you feel the need to make the rift in our family all about your mom's disease? You know too well that's not the case at all.*

Damn good question.

Thanks for asking.

### 2. The Life Raft

for 35 years I experienced our family as 98% love
2% occasional mild grouchiness
nobody's perfect, yet
you guys are to me

for the next 10 years, every day
I listened, watched, did battle
as Alzheimer's hacked away at Mom and Dad
both
I learned to accept powerlessness against it
that everything we've tried to help, will ever try, is shit
window dressing
arranging knickknacks, dusting bookshelves on the Titanic

Alzheimer's choked me, left me sobbing, sunk me,
tried to drown me
burned me more times than I can count
it burned me bare
I'm burning still and here I am
the essential intact, still grateful
Alzheimer's released the voice and the artist and the mother
and the father in my sister and me
restored the mermaids

instead of drowning us it is releasing us from fear
to become an entire ocean

returning more of our parents to us than we've ever known before
returning more of our planet to us than we could possibly have
received before

as ocean, we can reimagine anything, even Alzheimer's, as a Life
Raft

as ocean, we've pushed away those who hurt us
we accept that we've pushed you away, we don't blame you

as ocean, we've pulled toward us those who forgive and love us
flaws and all
we've pulled some relatives closer, wrapping them around us
warm blankets and fuzzy socks on bitter nights
we accept your anger at abandonment as our own

So, livid cousin, devastated aunt,
ghost uncles on whose behalf wicked-brave women speak to me
I am sorry for your pain and my part in it
I am sorry when you feel poetry as a cleaver in my hand or weight
around your neck
I am sorry when you experience me as a basher of family

that is not my intent
and I honor what you feel
I'll call myself a liar before I ever call you one

So why do I imagine Alzheimer's as a Life Raft now?

to hang on to you

as long as Alzheimer's holds its share of the blame
for this extended family rift —
holds my perspective too —
I don't have to lose you.

I don't have to lose you. You.

You.

Maybe I have to lose you for a little while, while we heal the rifts
within, but not forever.

Look again. At us. At what we're saying. At who we are. Where we are.

You will always be within my we. This we…

We are not exiled. We are not silent. We are not helpless. We are not liars. We are not orphans. We are not bashers of family. We have not been cut in half. None of us. That's our fear talking. Our fear. We are family.

We are poets and pilots.

We are parents and gardeners and farmers.

We are mermaids in matching pajamas.

We are the whole bloody ocean now.

When deeply wounded we can be cleavers.
We're both more vulnerable and more powerful than ever.

Nobody's perfect, yet
you guys are to me

### 3. Stupid Cleaver, You Missed Our Hearts Again

Alzheimer's disease
you meat cleaver
you hacker of brain and bone
you forest fire turning memory and limbs to ash
you can't get at these hearts

Alzheimer's disease you tried to exile us:
*I struggle to understand how any of this is the family's fault.*
(So do I. You are still my family. Hope I'm still yours.)

Alzheimer's disease you tried to accuse us:
*When you write about our family and how many walked away,*
*you know that's not true.*
(I walked away. Several of us did. We had to heal. We were bleeding. This is true for us. You are still our family. Hope we're still yours.)

Alzheimer's disease you tried to orphan and silence us:
*Writing about family that chose to distance themselves. No one chose*
*that. Everyone is reading it and in awe of the bashing.*
(I chose distance to repair and rebuild my broken heart. So did
my sister. Are we no one to you now? How is it that you still hear
us and we still hear you?)

Alzheimer's disease you tried to hack us clean in half:
*Your writing is warm and loving. Hang on tight to those* Berg *traits.*
(Those are Kane traits, too. I cannot be divided. I can't divide my-
self. Not even when people I love ask me to. Alzheimer's taught
me that. And you taught me that, family.)

Alzheimer's disease you hack out my eyes, blinding me, my ears,
deafening me, but somehow you keep missing my heart entirely:
*Had lawyers and judges not been introduced to our family none of*
*this would have happened and you know it. My God you make us*
*seem like heartless people who abandoned you and that hurts more*
*than anything. Her siblings would give anything to see her again and*
*you've chosen to blog about what a bunch of assholes we are. When it*
*all really comes down to that fucking court case.*
(Yes. For you it comes down to that. My heart expanded to hold
your truth when I allowed it to fully break. Yet even on the days
you rage at me for being me, your love is still there. My broken
heart sees yours. I am the last human on earth who would ever
call you heartless. So put that in your pipe and smoke it, ragey.
I'm so sad for our pain and loss that sometimes I have to step
away to mend. But not today. Today I welcome your pain and
rage. I envelop it. I am pain and rage now. Pain is my guide. Rage
is my bitch. So bring it. All of it. I will withstand your pain and
your rage. I will hug you tighter for them when I next see you. I
expect you'll do the same. We are not made of such fragile stuff as
we imagine, you and I.)

Alzheimer's disease you turned me into a writer of sad and dreary form letters:

Dear [*insert another family member who I love here*], I'm disconnecting from you for a year. I hope we can reconnect again later on. I learned today that the poem I wrote yesterday devastated you. I am sorry about that, it wasn't my intent. I am angry about a disease, and my own powerlessness in the face of it to stop it from destroying my parents. Rage is part of that. Rage is part of me now. This is me now. But blame isn't. I'm not angry at you guys. I don't hate you. I don't blame my family. I love you. For my own health, and my sister's, I need to write about our experience of Alzheimer's disease. Disconnecting temporarily allows me to do that without inadvertently hurting you again. If you need me for anything urgent this year, you can reach me at _____.
I look forward to reconnecting again in the future. I love you. – Lori

Alzheimer's disease, you fucking jerk
you made me the cleaver
there goes another of my precious limbs


4. Four Deep Breaths

## 5. Ocean

as your arms tire
day by day
release into me
drop cleavers in
sink blood-weary hands ever deeper
I have all the time in the world

I am ocean
we are mermaids
no leg to stand on among us

beyond words
beyond loss
beyond exile
beyond welcome

the essential
holds
our family
holds
us

those who cried this ocean with me
aren't anchors

you are my life raft

this we
here now

is my way home

## Needed to Breathe Deeply Right Now: Choose 1

blank page
empty space
a face turning into wind

solitude
bare feet
a fuck-it attitude

a friend's voice
removing my head from my own behind, again

felt freedom to mess up
keep learning

felt connection to the universe herself

nature before me
shifting from particle to wave

well-filled lungs
music

closed eyes
open eyes

receiving help from everything

sitting on the earth
walking
swimming

a good belly scream
true community

watching a silly cat video
aka, leaving an offering to the Internet gods

sobriety
levity
whispering yes and no repeatedly

expanding into frivolity

# Hate Within Me Now has a 3-Minute Shelf Life

We thought the Alzheimer's diagnosis would be hard.
Then, that the slow losing of Mom as we knew her
would be beyond hard.
These things seemed shatteringly difficult for so very many others.
How could we expect anything else?

But we're 10 years in now.
Now we know.
Those aren't the hard parts.

## I.

Alzheimer's strips away what doesn't matter right now,
exposing what does matter, to anyone fully present,
again and again,
much like the best
within schooling, science, religion,
philosophy, nature, art, comedy, parenting,
and house cleaning.
Strips away what doesn't matter. Reveals what does.
First, within her, then within us,
then within those who love us enough to move with us.

Sure, some days we expect to shatter.
But we actually don't. We ripple.
Alzheimer's is a stone
thrown onto a pond
shaking us as it sinks deeper
but if we move together
we don't shatter.

We are better for it, most days,
if we shift, turn into it,
pay closer attention
accept help
adjust our individual, our collective, selves.

Alzheimer's first stripped away her filters
so she always says exactly what's on her mind.
Sometimes it's painful, yes, and
sometimes it's fun, even hilarious.

Then it stripped away her boundaries,
so she greets and loves whomever she wants to now,
even strangers.
Turns on her heel, walking away from those she doesn't like,
without fuss, regret, or guilt.
It strips away our boundaries too.
We, too, now greet and love those we're meant to.
Walk, without guilt/regret/fuss, just like her,
away from situations that regularly cause us pain.

Then it stripped away independence:
hers, Dad's, ours, our closest others'
exposing our interdependence.
Good riddance extreme independence.
You are the most twisted, overrated value our country cranks out.
We are stronger now. More honest with ourselves, each other.
Explore depths across ourselves
we couldn't reach before.
The closer we get, the stronger we get,
the more truly independent we are.

Last year it washed away her fear of looking bad
exposing silliness and love and laughter at her core. Yes, and
that's rippling out into us now
for example, writer me becoming poet me,
my sister becoming a mother herself,
as our now-ridiculous fears wash out to sea with hers.

It strips away the illusion of control
requiring and allowing us
to prioritize ourselves
to create and re-create together
at times by the minute

a new response to this right now.
We're becoming improvisation masters,
just like her. She's our muse. Our center.
Like she's always been
always can be.

This year it's striping away the years
giving us a front row seat
to a gathering of people
we never imagined we'd meet.
To a mom at times in her forties, thirties, twenties
her teens
grade school
preschool.
This, because we're together, in itself, is not that hard.
Mom, at all stages, was, is
Happy. Loving. Curious. Helpful. Silly. Most of the time.
Cranky only when tired, and often not even then.
This is where the deeper blessings of our family reveal themselves.
Not all Alzheimer's families are this lucky.
Mom is happy, back then and right now, one, and the same.
And even luckier, on her darkest days, she still taps into empathy,
using it as a life line, sometimes better than the rest of us.
We are so so so amazingly lucky.
Good to remember when we find ourselves embarrassed
by her embrace of total strangers.

As we watch the stone
send ripples out across the pond,
it's quickly revealed
who our closest friends and family are:
who moves closer, with us, who moves farther away,
or is pushed away.
Those who move with us love all of us, no matter what,
are deep wellsprings of empathy,
bring out the best in us when we are at our worst,
have the courage to assume the best,
the ability to lead with forgiveness and kindness
no matter what.

What a tremendous gift in the face of fog and chaos:
to know exactly who your partners in crime are today,
and who aren't
to find solace, peace, even here
in the wake of departing loved ones.

II.

For us, what's hard about Alzheimer's isn't Alzheimer's.

What's hard is some people's response to it. For example:

1. Well-intentioned friends who show up to fix us,
instead of just being present, with us, here, open, hanging out,
improvising with us.
Yes, and
hello, that was me until Alzheimer's disease.

2. People who don't understand the disease's insidious impacts
to primary caregivers
who take bizarre new behavior, like silence or short-temperedness,
personally
who hate Dad for it.
We are sorry. And we are selective now about who we see
because we have to be or we'll shatter.
Hate him/us and you're out, for now.
Thanks to Alzheimer's we know this means just for now.
We hope you do to. We mean no offense.

3. Ourselves some days.
Sometimes we wallow in individual pain.
Forget the feelings of others.
We have to forgive ourselves more often now.
We grow weary. Make big mistakes.
We are becoming masters of forgiveness
because we have to be.
No choice.
To ripple not shatter,
we then open to growing closeness

because of shared pain
instead of chronically dwelling
on individual pain.
Otherwise we get stretched too thin
forget improvisation, how to love without limit.

4. A father/caregiver/husband
trying to do everything himself.
Fucking Greatest Generation
how I want to smack the lot of you some days.
Refusing to ask for or allow more caregiving help
for years.
Exhausting himself into a shell of his former self.
Living with his own chronic sicknesses.
Needlessly.
Doing way too much.
Needlessly.
Bringing forth his own sleeplessness, memory loss and confusion
bringing forth new stories of family pain as a result.
Reimagining extended family to highlight anger, erase love,
at times seeing monsters where nothing more than frightened
people exist
at times creating monsters
tilting at windmills preferable to receiving help.
And, far, far worse, that an exhausted man
manages to pull forth bad behavior from trusted others. Horrible.
I still can't believe he has that much influence in him.
Will he join us in rippling across the water?
Or will he shatter?
Too close to call.

5. People who try to mentally divide
our entirely undividable parents
trying to love and support
one half,
raising one up as a saint while insisting
the other is the devil incarnate.
Sorry, folks, there is no half here. We are whole.
Team Linda has become Team Jinda now.

All good. All crazy. All the time.
As are we,
with anyone brave enough
to stand with crazy-now us.
They are so whole, in fact,
that at times I wonder
if it will be easier for him to join her there –
walk into the lonely chaotic fog of memory-loss land –
than to watch her go there alone.

6. Distant, angry, attacking people anywhere
who judge from far away,
assume the worst of people instead of circumstances,
without firsthand understanding,
content to assume, blame, point fingers from afar,
instead of moving closer and connecting.
So goodbye politicians. Goodbye Internet trolls.
Goodbye chronic haters.
We literally don't have the time.
Yes, and
wow, that used to be me
content to stew and hate from a distance
before Alzheimer's.

Hate within me now has a 3-minute shelf life.

7. People who blame the primary caregiver
for "taking her away from us."
Please, for the love of God,
knock that shit off.
As if people who love her
could really be stopped
from seeing her, calling them, writing her,
visiting, sending care packages,
communicating with her somehow.

We communicate more now
than ever before,
even though most days,
she has very few words to work with.

They love visits, letters, cards, packages.
She needs a sidekick now
to stay on track
finish sentences and thoughts,
in person, on speakerphone, or Skype,
but she loves conversation (before 5 p.m.)
loves listening. Loves presence. Loves you.

I know it's scary. Seems impossible.
But it's not actually impossible for you, like it is for them.
You still have the gifts of time and letter writing,
of sending cards, little packages covered with doodles, or stickers.
Of having free time
being able to pick up a phone,
remember and dial numbers,
to reach out to someone you love. Of learning Skype
so you can see someone at a distance. Emailing.

Stop. Blaming. Others.
for your perfectly reasonable and acceptable decision
to step away for a while from
what you can't bear to see and hear right now.
A sleeping-half-the-day,
sick-all-the-time, shaky,
barely-holding-it-together,
74-year-old man
can be a major pain in the ass
but he is not the obstacle you imagine him to be.
Our own fear is.
Our own apparent inability
to do anything at all to kick Alzheimer's to the curb.
Our own inability
to change what IS into what WAS.

Dad's in no position anymore to bat away hands
outstretched in love.
But we are in a position to love
even in the face of anger and rage at being lonely,
destined to fail to save the love of your life,

at having to grieve every damn day.
For 15 years (no wait, 5 now, if we're lucky).
WE are not powerless now. Just the opposite.
We are being asked to become stronger
more powerful than we were.
Accept what is. Channel anger into something good.
Step out in courage! Be more persistent!
More fucking loving than ever before!
She would for us if she could.
And you may never believe us now, but, if he could:
So. Would. He.
You may never forget that you
turned your back on them in return.
I really don't want that for you. We love you.

8. And to the family member
content to periodically yell
at my pregnant sister
for not adequately fixing
our evil father
while she's working with him to feed Mom, dress Mom,
bathe Mom,
noticing his closed, tired eyes,
hands shaking from his own non-stop coughing,
from forgetting to eat.
Watching him fall asleep mid-sentence, mid-joke,
mid-conversation,
because he's been awake every hour, all night again, with Mom.
Watching Mom bring him his pills, with water,
because he only has the energy
to help her remember to always take hers regularly
at times forgetting his own.

STOP venting at my sister.

Bring your anger your pain your frustration
your deepest rage
to me now.
I will hear you for her.
She needs a break.

Honor this request
or you might step on her heart so completely that you'll lose her.
Completely.
I doubt you will. But I'd rather not take that risk
with her heart or yours.

## III.

Alzheimer's never asks us what we want. Doesn't give us a choice.
Not those of us really close to her.
Here in the heart of it
we must get closer to people who want to connect and help,
drop pretense,
reveal vulnerabilities,
move through pain together.
We must get on with the business of loving who we love
letting go of people and things and places
we don't have the energy for right now.
When we don't, we shatter.

We shatter.

She gives us
no choice.

FUCK THIS DISEASE! FUCK THAT WE REGULARLY
LOSE PEOPLE — A FUCKING LOT OF PEOPLE FROM
OUR LIVES IT TURNS OUT — BECAUSE OF IT!

FUCK THAT FAILURE TO SAVE MOM IS OUR ONLY
CERTAINTY! FUCK THAT WE FAILED TO KEEP OUR
WHOLE FAMILY TOGETHER THROUGH THIS! FUCK
EARLY ONSET ALZHEIMER'S THAT GIVES JEN AND I
CONSTANT DAILY REMINDERS THAT WE MAY GET
THIS DISEASE AND PUT OUR HUSBANDS AND LOVED
ONES THROUGH FUCKING ALL OF THIS AGAIN IN A
FEW YEARS!

FUCK FUCK FUCK!*

*Hmm, I may be more at risk for Tourette's than Alzheimer's. ;-)

# IV.

Ok, so we shatter
we fall completely apart
yes, and
here we are
still ripples in the same pond.
We're still us.
Still the pond.

You don't scare me now, shatter, you ratty little weasel.

Bring it.

Because

Wow are we learning how to love right now, flaws and all.
Flaws are where we connect. We love flaws!

Wow are we deeply grateful for tiny little things,
the smallest kindnesses.
That sunshine against your cheek? A gift.

Wow can we move fluidly, together, with exquisite grace.
Laughing.
Without words. Like geese and jazz musicians.

Wow can we get through anything, forgive anything,
including ourselves.

What?! We can now control how long hate stays within us?
Aware that it is our choice and that this too-short life is precious?

We can choose seconds or minutes with hate
and not be stuck with it for months or years?
We can save our energy/selves/family/love/world from you?

I had no idea we were this powerful.

I choose 3 minutes with hate now, out of habit. Take that, silly
hate, stupid shatter.

What?! We can have fun now
the deepest fun we've ever had
Any where? Any time?

We can walk up to anyone?! Hug, with true connection,
whomever we want to hug?!
Good God. The whole earth is our playground.

I find myself happy to be Alzheimer's student.

I find myself happy to be her student, most days**.
**See FUCK FUCK FUCK above.

I'm happy to spend time in her company
among others here
people who are willing to move into exhaustion
and anger and rage
visibly
who come back out again, this time holding hands and smiling.

Our rag-tag Alzheimer's improv troupe
is learning that the way to keep things moving
is to respond with "Yes! And..."
to what IS right now
to the worlds created by our companions,
whether or not we understand or agree
or think their world has any ground or truth
in our reality.

We're learning to expand their world and ours,
by weaving our worlds together in real time
co-creating new worlds within which all of our perspectives
and responses are valid, proper, and true.

Today – more than 10 years into Alzheimer's – Mom is a master
of world weaving.
The Dalai Lama of improv.
While the rest of us just try to keep up.

It can be frustrating to encounter people who can't really
see us now,
can't improvise with us right now

especially loved ones we used to count on.
But except for being tired and scared at times, ourselves,
we have no reason to bear anyone ill will
not anymore.

If we step away from you
we're just not ready right now
to have our world expanded by yours.
Or you're not quite ready to see us
as we truly are
right now.

V.

We have become a river.

We aren't what we used to be.

Some people fear us now. We live with that.

Some love us more than ever: closer and reminded that
we're still us, still here

loving to laugh, cry, and hang out.

Belting out Sisters from White Christmas
sillier and sexier than ever.

Inventing brand new music as we go.

You just have to be willing to see more of us now
willing to say "Yes! And…"
willing to believe that you, too,
if you step toward us
will survive the chaos, survive the shatter
to come out playing together
on the other side.

# Stop Preaching Forgiveness to the Drowning

*a poem for me*

When you see a woman drowning
don't ask her to forgive the man beside her
throwing anchors in her direction.

You may be able to see that he is drowning too.
She can't. Plus,
forgiving him now will actually kill her.

Trust her deeper wisdom in this moment
her instinct to turn away.

For the love of God
stop preaching forgiveness to the drowning
when our only immediate options are turning away
or throwing anchors back and forth
until we drown.

# Through the Flames, Watch for Deep Grace

*What is an essay doing in book of poetry? I don't know. What can I say? It demanded to be here. I've let go of the belief that I'm the boss of these poems and essays. They do what they want. I work for them.*
– Lori

Turning away from the deepest suffering means turning away from the deepest grace. That's the heart of this essay.

Several friends and I have asked ourselves the same question this past year:

> How do I keep an open heart
> while standing in the depths
> of pain, of suffering, of hell?

Everybody's answer is slightly different.

As a new poet, my answer has been to surround myself with other poets and writers who've done the same. This year especially, as my family and I fell into our own personal mini-hell, I've turned to black poets, black writers, and other voices that stay with extraordinary pain, creating through it, pulling forth stunning creation and broken-open, stunning, badass new selves. Work that other broken-hearted, angry, and frightened people can stay with and feel. Or willingly return to, when they're stronger. Broken, weeping people, like me.

The voices of black poets, especially, have pushed me along this year when I thought the pain of my family would shatter me. They surrounded me when it did shatter me. They celebrated with me when I came out the other side a new creature: stronger, gentler, fiercer, kinder, beautiful: a voice forged in fire.

Staying with pain, standing in the fire, in your own hell, is horrible. It is horrific. Words fail. There is screaming and yelling and crying and rage and grieving and mourning and exhaustion and not getting out of bed and cowering and hiding and giving up entirely. The only true words that can emerge at this point are: "This is hell. I am in hell."

I've learned to listen to voices that have lived through and spoken those words. And to those who've died and had others speak those words on their behalf. They were my saviors this year in many ways.

It can take a long time to get to these words. Yet, once spoken, the words "This is hell." can bring forth a new self. One cracked open to and receiving deeper insight, growth, clarity, strength, peace, friendship, and grace. Ridiculously deep grace. Grace that pre-hellfire you couldn't even imagine.

Suffering is horrible. You have to let it be what it is: horrible. Name it. Face it. Fall apart.

Then, not before, you can become more graceful. Falling apart is important. It allows suffering to move through you instead of pooling and stagnating within you. Suffering can become a tremendous gift when we're ready. A tremendous gift to a community or a country when we're ready.

We're ready.

In Ferguson. At the center of this United States in November in 2014. At the center of our collective, unspoken, ignored, stagnating and sinking-us hell.

To my ear, saying that black lives matter is not saying that the lives of law enforcement officers don't matter. It's the opposite. It's a reminder to those of us still avoiding our pain to wake up, see the fire we're all standing in, and remember that black lives matter to all of us. Remember that black children's lives matter. That watching black children die in the street, and anywhere else, has been breaking our collective heart again and again and again in this country for a long time now. That killing hurts everyone. Much of white America is ready to listen now. The repeated, pointless, death of person after person after person in this country has pulled us into our own hell. All of us. This searing pain and fear and anger when another person is killed for holding cigarettes or toys or candy, or walking or driving down the wrong street, or just looking at somebody the wrong way? And they're killed for it?

This. This is what hell feels like.

To my ear, which now contains my heart, people saying black lives matter are saying this:

This is hell. I am in hell. We are in hell. Talk to me. Work with me. Help in whatever way you can before our whole country burns to the ground on the backs of dead children.

Hard to hear. Hard to say. Hard to write.

And not everyone is ready to hear and say these words, even now. But I am.

I've been through my own hell this year, and I find that it's much easier to listen now, to face hell, and to speak. I don't have to turn away from suffering to find grace. Grace is always here.

I can stand with those in hell right now. #BlackLivesMatter

When I take that stand, I can bear the loss of friends who cannot bear to even look at where I'm standing right now. I can take their anger, fear, rage, and disgust. And I can receive them when they choose to return.

I can stand with the vulnerable. With those who walk together, unarmed, terrified, with little hope, yet moving anyway, for the sake of their neighbors, children, family, and selves. People throwing their whole being/community/country onto the fire for everyone's sake, not just their own. Because they know we'll be better for it.

I can stand with those who have stood in the heart of their own hell, burned, shattered completely, and stepped forth new people, willing and able to speak for those who no longer have a voice.

Wow, do they move with grace.

There are hundreds of links available now to find and follow if you have the courage and space within you to do something in response to what you know is happening in Ferguson right now. My dear journalist friend shared this one — 12 Things White People Can Do Now Because Ferguson — specifically for those unaccustomed to stepping into the fire of racism and white supremacy at all, let alone together. Google it.

This essay is for people who can't do anything right now. People caught up in their own mini-hells, for example, too exhausted and sad and beaten down and scared to extend care out beyond the smallest of circles yet. I get it. I've been there. So recently that my tears aren't even dry yet.

I ask one small thing, for your own sake. If you cannot bear to act or look at Ferguson right now, please don't look entirely away. Instead, look for those in the heart of the fire who move with the deepest grace. They are there. Look closer or ask someone to look for you and report back. Chaos will organize itself around them. Watch and notice that even chaos bows before deep grace. Everything else becomes background noise.

Watch for those moving with deep grace in the heart of hell. Watch and learn. They will teach you how to keep your heart open within the deepest suffering and pain. How to survive your own hell.

You need that deep grace now more than ever. We all do.

Don't look away.

# 3. Exploring the Connections among Gifting, Generosity, and Generativity

# Poems as Generative Gifts

This section contains poems that I created as gifts for specific people: both flash and regular poems that I took my time with. Here *flash poetry* means any poem created for and gifted to someone specific less than 10 minutes after the inspiration to create a poem for them surfaced within me. I wasn't fully conscious that I was regularly creating flash poetry this year until I look back across my blog posts and Facebook posts for the year and saw that I'd rapidly created and gifted quite a few poems for people I love and also for total strangers. Except for reading about a few poets who sit in parks and type out poems on old typewriters for lucky passersby, flash poetry isn't something I knew about ahead of time, or studied, or mimicked, or consciously tried to do at all. I just did it for the fun of it and when I felt compelled to.

I have been living and working as part of the gift economy for many years now. Maybe it was my lucking into a generous family. Maybe it was my choosing to host free coworking spaces within my communities. Or maybe it was that my communities promoted gifting. Or my mom's Alzheimer's disease, which pulls forth generosity from everybody. Or something else entirely. I'm not certain. But I now live in a world where people show up with gifts, give gifts, receive gifts, and are, themselves, gifts most days. And maybe if this is the world you live in, and you become a poet, then gifting poetry to people the moment they need it isn't strange at all. To me it's like a farmer giving vegetables or a parent giving hugs. Flash poetry is just something I intuitively do.

There are several really cool things about flash poetry. The speed at which you work tends to suck ego and worry-spinning out of the process faster than normal. All raw materials are fair game—photos, feelings, your things, other people's things, anything you happen upon in the moment really—which is just fun. And maybe the best part is that flash poems are allowed to suck. Whether the poem is good, bad, perfect, terrible, or otherwise, it is the act of giving the poem itself that touches people. In my experience, flash poetry is gratefully received by the person it was created for, which lifts the spirit and builds confidence within both receiver and poet (perhaps especially within a new poet, clearly still learning). The only voice that matters in flash poetry beyond your own is that first person who received it as a gift to begin with. The person whose eyes and heart lit up in the receiving of it: "You wrote *me* a poem? Wow." No expert or critic or editor or fear can take that experience away from you. Ever.

Flash poetry got me into the habit of gifting poems to people when they need them. I went on to create and share longer poems with people who really seemed to need them. Many of those same poems turned around and became gifts for me when I was struggling in my own life. Strange how that works. Good strange. Unlike tacky knickknacks, there's no taboo against poetry re-gifting. In fact, poems give themselves whenever, and to whomever, they please without fear, thought, or regret.

Poems are already living the lives that we ourselves hope to live. How wonderful.

# On Marrying a Poet

*flash poetry for my husband Daniel*

Chris Toll said
The job of poets is not to explain the Mystery.
The job of poets is to make the Mystery greater.

Terrific, said Daniel, but my question was:
where do you want to eat dinner
tonight?

# Gunman Me

*flash poetry for Sabina Giado*


She showed up in my newsfeed after the shooting
saying the wisest of things:

"We all really need to examine ourselves and
think about what separates us from these gunmen.
Patience. Compassion. Humility. Humanity.
Will we give those values up when pushed? Food 4
thought."

Excellent food for thought
like somebody mixed kale and chocolate chip cookies
performed a miracle
made a good meal.

In response, first my brain threw forth a word:

poverty!

Then I argued with myself:

but that can imply a lack of money,
which doesn't feel like the true difference to me,
most of the kind people I know — especially the
young now —are financially poor — and they're the most
generous people I know

My soul volunteered a thought:

No, I meant a poverty of people.

a complete lack of listening humans

present to listen
present to help me feel noticed, heard, of value

Then it hit me:

Fully present people are all that separates right-now me
from gunperson-me.

"There but for the grace of God, go I."
I heard my grandmothers and mother say within me.

"There but for the grace of Sabina," I responded.
"Goes gunman me."

Sabina said

"I see what you're saying.
We need to fortify those distinctions within ourselves
however we can, even if it means
valuing and listening to ourselves.
It's hard. I'm still learning how to self-love."

Ouch. My heart broke. Soul reeled:

How can self-love be hard
for this funny, thoughtful, amazing human?
She's so loveable that even a total stranger can feel it.

I first said this:

We're all still learning, I think.
Might even be why we're here.
To support each other in learning to love ourselves.

Then I wrote some #micropoetry. Because
to think and speak isn't enough anymore, is it?

　　while you may struggle
　　to love yourself
　　for me
　　already
　　loving you
　　just feels like
　　breathing

minds find refuge in silence
bodies find refuge in presence

what sounds surround us?

the silence of presence
weeping and laughter
wind in the tree tops
water above us
souls harmonizing

and
nothing
more

# From the Women Who Called Forth the Muse

*flash poetry for Steph Kent*

Amidst yet another abstract conversation
among the wisest of men
Steph showed up fully
asking:

I'd be interested,
if you're game to share,
what you found after the failure of forgiveness?

Oh!
lovely witness
question
muse
you

Thank you for asking.

I said Hmm
I felt emptiness
letting go
lightness: a weight lifted, gravity shifted
rest
peace
quiet
getting to know a new me
new eyes
toddling around on small shaky feet
then new stories
new energy, new power.
I became a mermaid, then a dragon.

much unexpectedly later one day
sipping peppermint tea
in my deep velvet blue chair
forgiveness was just there, like cat hair

Not commanded or demanded or even wanted.
always present
stuck to my socks and gray pants
tiny halos of stubborn presence

The wisest of men
showed back up again
something about us having strayed off topic
but, like always, the men were just a moment too late

The muse was present.

she swept us up in a wind that wrapped
around a distant star
so by the time they tried to ground us
we could only see starlight
could only hear ourselves:
the wind, the muse
the questions, the response

and the women
calling everything forth

# Voice of a Leader

*flash poetry for my friend Jeffrey David Zacko-Smith, Leadership Professor (among many other wonderful things). Just for giggles one day, I turned undecipherable student prose, which was driving him crazy, into a poem for him...*

And

when discussing
qualities of
effective leaders

So

many people
list
communication
balance
being authentic
walking your talk
many people

And
So

many others.

It just gets confusing
to someone

someone

to me.

How do I
become a leader
when all I hear
is voices?

How do I
silence the many voices
and find my own?

# Loving to Pieces, Autopoiesis

*Flash poetry for my amazingly prolific and resilient researcher friend Giorgio Bertini. I turned a research abstract he shared into a poem on the fly for him. That's me, apparently: extremely nerdy poems on the fly, no waiting.*
*Isn't life beautiful?*

emergence
resurgence
convergence

moving away
some days
from reduction mind-sets
to dance
with holist approaches

honoring context
squeezing self-organizing systems
loving to pieces, autopoiesis
misty-eyed chaotic systems
tickling multi-agent systems
blushing

running across the field
lighting up aspects and helpers
in understanding emergence

falling down laughing with stories
research and measures
bringing forth
emergent performance
flexibility
to greet agent organization
at your own dawn

researcher releasing
becoming
creator

coming
home

# Within the Unknowing

*A poem created for neighbors Scott and Rachelle, as we wait-*
*ed in agony, for weeks, for word about Bailey — daughter,*
*neighbor, friend — missing in Langtang Valley, Nepal after*
*the earthquake. Strangely, the same day I shared this with*
*them, my sister Jen went into labor several states away from*
*me. As the hours passed and I didn't hear from Jen, I began*
*to panic and ended up re-reading this poem a few times for*
*myself and my sister. Sometimes poems and prayers become*
*indistinguishable.*


within the unknowing
we offer unwavering presence
tell your stories, our stories
so many inside giggles

within the unknowing
at times we keep busy
searching, sharing, worrying
gardening, cooking, praying, offering

sometimes we grow weary, angry
within the unknowing
falter, weep, recover
all responses are ok here, just fine
we're learning what rest is
how to shelter in place within life herself
drop what doesn't matter to be held by what does

within the unknowing
love is everything, distance nothing
we touch the same earth comforted
look at the same sky smiling
aware of being loved by each other
known each moment of our existence
treasured by every molecule of the planet

within the uncertainty
we see you, hold you, know you
float within unknowing together
certain of nothing but each other
at times surprised to find ourselves laughing, even now
because to know you fills us so completely

like always
and always

# The Return

*As I mentioned earlier, my extended family shattered this past year. At one point, I cut ties with several family members for a year so that we could rest, heal, and not move past anger into contempt. I created this poem for the family members I was saying goodbye to. Because I never stopped loving them and I wanted them to know — like I knew, even as we parted — that they will always be welcome to return to our home.*

## I.

Goodbye family who cannot bear the weight of me.
Goodbye family whose deep pain my own frame cannot bear.

We hung on for so long to outdated expectations
to what we used to be
failing each other, sinking our intertwined souls
until it sickened, almost killed
our right-now selves.
Thank God for chocolate.

Goodbye family

It says something remarkable about what we used to be
that we held on to old hopes and selves for so long

It says something more remarkable about what we are now
that we chose to breathe deep and let go here

Goodbye

We're finally free
to love what we still have more deeply
push away what no longer serves us
pull new love toward us
connect with other broken hearts better suited to heal our own.

## II.

Hello love

I love the faces that show up to listen and say "me too"
I love the earth that steadies my feet,
the thick fuzzy socks that warm them
I love the bed, inviting judgement-free comfort zone,
for the reminder
I love the cocoa for its short, sweet glimpse at days gone by

I love the power in the simplest of words now:
PJs rock. Fuck pants today.

I love the gathering power within.

I love the sky even more now
where thoughts float
among stars and words drop in like neighbors
I love neighbors
who stop by unannounced without words
like rock stars

I love that the sun never fails to warm my face
when I turn toward her.
I love that the family still beside me, smiling, able to cry my tears,
has become more powerful than the sun.

Hello love

I'm so glad we set down the weight of our own expectations to
race across the sand with the dog. Yes, I was wearing pajamas.

I'm so glad we moved within pain
to greet the new self approaching.
This broken-hearted, love-rich, weeping bad ass.
This never-not-broken goddess, sleepy and tireless,
strong and vulnerable
defender of broken-hearted people and their worlds.

I'm so glad we all remember with body-deep clarity
what a loving family feels like.

I'm thrilled that none of us settles for less
for ourselves and those we love.
I love that you have so much strength and fight left in you
that you'll be just fine, free and rising, without us.

III.

Goodbye family, I love you.

Thank you for teaching me to love
when I was little.

Thank you for learning with me
now that we're grown
that we won't settle for less
from anyone.

Thank you for bravely pulling forth your unspoken
so I could see it.

IV.

The girl you knew
Drowned
in a sea of frustration, half-truths,
rage, fear, and assumptions.
She is dead.
Mourn her as long as you need to.
Then let her go.

V.

When you are ready, come

Come greet the woman
who steps toward you from the sea
laughing, wounded, new, content, scarred, and whole.
Sacred truths shatter around her. She doesn't.
(Ok, sometimes she does before she rises.)
Love never leaves her presence.
She's a wellspring of love because love shows up in others,
surrounds her

pours into her when she's nearing empty
and she lets it all in

She loves messiness and openness. Leaves sand on the floor.
Dishes go unwashed for days sometimes.
She sleeps late. Visiting friends learn to make their own breakfast.
She's been seen walking barefoot in the sand, even in winter.
She pulls rainbows out of the darkest sky
from bed, in her pajamas, while crying.

She may be strange but she's not a stranger.
She has her mother's smiling eyes.
She may be fierce sometimes
and there's absolutely nothing to fear within her.
Her father's strength.

You will find rest and welcome at her shore.
Bring comfy pajamas. Wash your own dishes. Forgive.
And you'll be invited to return.

# Second Wife

*Another poem for Daniel. God help him.*

Dear spouse,

I want to tell you about grief. No, I don't.
I want to tell you about me – the woman emerging from the
ocean in winter, naked.
The wife you loved and knew died in my arms yesterday.
You'll be living with me now: Wife 2.0. Lucky man.

First the good news.

I couldn't care less where you leave your socks and shoes.
Don't care when or if you ever do your dishes.
I think weeds are lost, misunderstood yard angels.
That sand on the floor should be sculpted i
nto intricate art installations
at least as often as it is mindlessly swept away.
I enjoy wearing the same cozy sweater
for days on end while I create
I don't like doing laundry.
Stains are more misunderstood angels
ideal brooch locations.

Crap. Maybe that was the bad news. Let me try again.

First the good news.

When you can't find me
I might be on the beach looking at rocks
on my hands and knees
tumbling words in my poet's mind
like the most devoted lapidarist.
Words are cool. Rocks contain words for those who look.

Most days you'll find me at my writing desk.
Epic tales in pajamas. Poems everywhere.

When life really sucks
you might find me reading strange books, watching strange TV
last month I watched all 153 episodes of The Gilmore Girls
on Netflix, in rapid succession, to mend my heart
when my extended family shattered.
I feel no shame. No guilt.
All my experience is gift. All of it.
Rory and Lorelai were there when grief burned my branches bare.
Silly, imperfect help is plenty.
You won't catch this wife judging your taste in entertainment.
Our hearts know who and what they need to heal.

I offer one tip.

Don't worry about me. Just don't.
Some days I may appear lost and alone.
That's part of me. A part I love.
Being lost and alone rocks most days.

I am an explorer. I take my time.
I move through The Museum of Modern Loss with wonder
Whoa. What? Huh. Wow.
pain and grief are just T-Rex bones in the rotunda.
Vulnerabilities are just strengths that I widened to
reveal, revel in, more of me.
When my skin gets too small I move toward them
crack myself open to step through new. Whole.
Doesn't make me a chicken. Or a dinosaur.
When I need rest, I take it (see *The Gilmore Girls*, above).
Or I get a wrist guard. Or I ask for help.

This wife asks for help when she needs it. Let me ask.

Ok, that was two tips. Now the bad news.

You're married to an artist now.
Living a textbook case for use of the expression "Man up."
Artists pull forth new worlds. Find comfort in chaos.
Stand still at the heart of hell to burn, listen,
record for remembrance. Chase fireflies.

Our hands our heads our hearts all equals
This makes us absentminded some days. Messy most.
My train even more choo choo – tough to – follow that thought
Fully engage your heart to hear me now. And your funny bone.
And your home-keeping skills. And your improv skills.

An artist will not try to engage parts of you for you.
That's on you.
I am engaged with myself.

Shit. Maybe that was the good news. You tell me.

Grieve her in your way, as you must.
You knew her well, that woman
the one inclined to weep over shoes and rage about dirty dishes.

I can't.

The gifts of rage and weeping will not be wasted
on dust and cutlery in this house.

Screw it, honey, the dishes will keep.

Today we dance.

# 4. Receiving the Gift of Free Moments

# Being a Poet in the Land of the Busy

I do my damnedest to not be busy. I don't believe in busy. I believe in the slow life. The good life. In synchronizing life and work to the seasons and the tides whenever possible. I believe with all my heart (and experience) that I do my best for this world when I live and work in non-busy land. Many months, I actually pull this off. Other times, I fail. And sometimes — such as this fall — I fail spectacularly…

I anticipated that fall of 2015 would be relatively quiet. I mean, yes, I would be publishing two books, and doing annual home canning with neighbors, but these aren't new processes for me. I know how to do these things and they're fun. Beyond that, I'd cleared my calendar really well. So well, in fact, that for fun I signed up for my friend's 6-month online writer's workshop. So my slow life = good life fall was all nicely imagined into place. Then a whole lot of real life happened…

My sister had a baby — hurray! My first niece needed visiting and snuggling.

A new friend showed up and asked me to help start a community coworking space here on the island like I'd done before in Seattle. Fun!

Then another new friend asked if I'd join a memory and brain wellness center board where I could use what my family has learned about living with dementia to support other families doing the same. Yes! What an honor! Of course!

Then my on-the-waiting-list parents received word that a cottage had become available in their new 55+ community here on Whidbey: five months ahead of schedule. Suddenly, they needed considerable help setting up a new home from scratch here, moving their car (and some other things) here, connecting with local doctors, banks, etc. I love my parents and I can't wait for them to finally be closer. Hooray! Yet, all of a sudden, things began feeling busy. Then, as my dad would say, the shit hit the fan…

Daniel was unexpectedly laid off from his day job of 9 years. Just like that: there went 90% of our income.

We made the decision to attempt to actually make a living as a full-time writer and photographer team. Two-years ahead of schedule. Yay! And, ah, yikes. Scary.

We simultaneously made the decision to sell our Seattle home, since we know that making a full living as artists will be a multi-year process. All of a sudden we had meetings with a real estate agent, asking friends to move out of our Seattle home, scheduling and overseeing a dozen contractors doing maintenance/repair/beautification projects at the Seattle house, and doing countless small projects there ourselves as well. Dozens of Seattle neighbors showed up to have goodbye talks and dinners with us. And did I mention that we had to drive 90+ minutes to and from Seattle each day from Whidbey Island to make that happen?

By mid-October, I was well past busy. I was overwhelmed. We had to make a 65-line-item spreadsheet just to keep track of this work. Yuck! My body began aching from all the physical labor we were doing (I told myself). The truth is, I was aching from the stress of doing too much.

At the same time, I began researching employment agencies thinking that — come January — I would pick up a 3- to 6-month contract gig to have some extra money and a regular paycheck for a while so that we could refinance our Whidbey house. But the same day I mentioned on Facebook that I was researching area employment agencies, multiple friends asked me if I'd like to do technical writing and editing work for them. Yay! And, could I start immediately? Holy shit. Umm, ah, sure?!

What kind of idiot decides to publish two books, sell a house, help parents move, help create a new small business, help start a coworking space, join a new board, take a new class, and start a new full-time job *in the same month*? That would be me.

Lori and busy are like Oprah and weight loss. We keep learn-ing, it seems. Keep getting wiser, it seems. And yet just when we suspect we've got it all figured out our demons return to haunt us.

Despite appearances, though, I really have been learning. I pulled off living in non-busy land for a long time this last time, and something has shifted within me I notice...

A few minor FMLs (Fuck My Life!) aside this month, I learned that I don't mind it here in busy land as much as I used to.

I know it's not forever. That helps. And most of the things I said Yes! to bring me deep joy (e.g., sister visit, coworking, joining the coolest board ever, publishing books, helping parents, working with Daniel, and not being a landlord anymore). That helps too.

Beyond that, I fiercely hung on to walks with the dog (and now Daniel) in the wilderness and stolen moments of writing each day as if my life depended on them. That really helped.

I've learned to embrace anger this year. That really helped. For example, I embraced my anger at the way Daniel was treated by an employer he trusted: fully felt it for a while, shared it with friends, and moved with it so that it could pass on through me instead of pooling within me.

I hung on to laughing with Daniel about how utterly crappy things were at points — for example, after a week of sunrise to midnight work on our home as we stood in our Seattle basement, dusty, exhausted, and waist deep in the left-behind furniture, household goods, food, and garbage of roughly 20 former house-mates and cottage renters. I barely cried at all when the Dump It guys told us we'd need to order a second truck and come back to Seattle yet another day because we'd overfilled their truck.

So we tried something new for us: bad mood days. Have you done this? During the worst, busiest, most exhausting days, we decided "These next few days are just going to be crappy. We have way too much to do. We are already exhausted. And this has to be finished in the next 3 days. So these are officially be-as-snippy-as-you-want-and-when-you-want-to-be-snippy days." What a relief to just be able to be visibly exhausted and grumpy and pissed off for a while. Together.

In years past, faced with a similar waterfall of changes in a short span of time, one of the first things I would remove from my too-full plate was my own writing. You know, the one thing that without fail always gives me energy, calms me down, provides free therapy, cheers me up, and feels like me actually getting to be fully me. In the past I would prioritize family, friends, community, coworking space, partner, pets, home, and coworkers in times of too busy or chaos. I would drop myself.

Thanks to poetry, I no longer drop myself.

This year — even during the worst times — I prioritized myself and my writing. I finally saw how important I am to myself/family/friends/community/partner/pets/home/coworkers. Some days this year, I succeeded in prioritizing huge chunks of writing time. Other days, like this fall, I only had 10 minutes to write. Or 5 minutes. Or 1 minute. Or 30 seconds.

But even in these brief moments, now, I keep writing. I keep right on being me…

Enter Micropoetry. Enter Six Word Story. Enter online poeting-for-the-fun-of-it groups. Enter itty bitty self-publishing on Twitter and Facebook where others can see what I write. Enter writing in beach sand and on car windows and grocery receipts and rocks and in old notebooks where the writing is just for me and the sky.

Enter reading short poems out loud to other poets and neighbors now and then. Learning to read poetry through tears in public without apologizing for my tears.

Enter feeling like Emily Freaking Dickenson in the middle of days when the rest of my life is in chaos. Yay! And with this feeling, I am living the slow life, the good life, again. Right here. Right now. Within the chaos. One 30-second moment after the next…

This poetry is truly entirely just for me — me! — on days I'm barely holding it together or days when 30 seconds is all I have.

# Micropoetry

within the busy
within the chaos
deep within Fuck My Life!
thank you
#Micropoetry

for helping me
hold on to me

*first published September 28, 2015*


I see your breath
in the cool fall air
imagine you a dragon
free
belonging to none
flying home to me
#micropoetry

*first published September 27, 2015*


Eva Louise, Eva Louise
fuzzy dimpled puppy knees
goes outside
brings in fleas
that's the tail
of Eva Louise
#micropoetry

*first published September 4, 2015*

I breathe
I write
I sleep
laugh, mourn, weep
No because.
Just creation and always.
#womenwrite

*first published August 8, 2015*
*in response to @WomenWriters asking "Why do you write?*
*#womenwrite"*


love the sky
where thoughts float among stars & words
drop in like neighbors

love neighbors
who stop by unannounced like rock stars
#micropoetry

*first published July 30, 2015*


much unexpectedly later one day
sipping peppermint tea in my deep velvet blue chair
forgiveness was just there, like cat hair
#micropoetry

*first published July 13, 2015*

within the slanted evening shade
I feel a soft deer presence

before I see her

in stillness I know myself magic
she sees it too
#micropoetry

*first published June 29, 2015*

My answer to the question
"What do you want to be when you grow up?"
Wilderness.
I want to be wilderness.
#micropoetry

*first published June 25, 2015*


I love telling people I'm a poet.
They have no idea what it means
except that they should be the one to pick up the check.
#poets #poetslife

*first published May 6, 2015*


She crinkles eyes
tickles toes'
helps lost dogs
smells the roses
crafts new books
cans new jams
finds abundant worlds
within the sand
#npm

*published April 15, 2015 for National Poetry Month
(during which I played with writing a poem a day for the
fun of it)*

drowning in the shallow ideas sea
she turned and faced the ocean
stepped in
set herself adrift
remembered herself swimming
#micropoetry #NPM

*first published April 11, 2015*


impatient springtime
pollen & passion
show up 2 embrace her

beware too-clean windows
knocking yourself out
in sun-dripping delirium
#poetry

*first published April 8, 2015*


too much work
not enough play
and your poet self
just flies away
#micropoetry #PoetryMonth

*first published April 2, 2015*


everywhere I go these days I find my people
and they are beautiful
#poets

*first published February 19, 2015*

while you may struggle
to love yourself

for me already
loving you
just feels like breathing
#micropoetry

*first published February 11, 2015*


puppyhood:
a spiritual practice
designed to help us get over a lot of shit
#micropoetry

*first published January 25, 2015*


earthquake!
the chaos
the mess

dreadful stinking stupid bloody earthquake

beauty arising
being within chaos
release
more space for me
beautiful you

have you noticed your own beauty rising yet?

*first published January 20, 2015*
*inspired by an complex image that an earthquake created*
*in fine sand*

even with a sore ass
I find myself
content.

that's poetry
#micropoetry

*first published December 30, 2014*


Ah, book marketing.
You are the diaper contents of my new born baby. ☺
#micropoetry

*first published December 2, 2014*

# Six Word Stories

Your artist self will save you.

#NaMoSix

*First published October 28, 2015*

*in response to Susan Jensen's prompt on the Whidbey Authors Facebook page "Best writing advice… in six words."*

Shaking hands with what's behind me...

#amwriting #sixwordstory

*first published August 25, 2015*
*in response to @WriterlyTweets' prompt "In six words or fewer, write a story about what you find after walking through a mirror. #amwriting #sixwordstory"*

Not quiet:
just communicates
via books.

#sixwordstory

*published June 17, 2015 in response to @Hedgebrook's writing prompt: "In SIX WORDS or fewer, tell us what your warning label would be. #SixWordStory"*

His sugar mama preferred pressed pajamas.

#sixwordstory #amwriting

*first published June 9, 2015 in response to @WriterlyTweets'*
*prompt: "In six words or fewer, write a story about a wealthy*
*suitor. #amwriting #sixwordstory"*

# 5. Following Curiosity

# Curiosity Doesn't Kill Readers and Poets

As I looked back across the poetry I wrote in the last year, there were four clear responses answering the question "Where does poetry come from?" A question this second-year poet is still figuring out. Honestly, I suspect I'll return to this question often across my life. It's such a fun question.

My clear responses to this question this year were: 1) moving with reverence, 2) staying with pain, 3) gifting and generativity, and 4) receiving the gift of free moments. Yet not all the poetry fell neatly into those four buckets. I was left with a bunch of quirky, misfit poems that didn't fully fit into these themes, and it wasn't obvious how, or if, they related to each other at all.

The poems in this section made me wonder, look longer, and reflect more deeply about my own experiences and process. Viva la misfits! Viva la disruptors! What finally came to me was a treat because I'd never noticed it before: curiosity. All these poems showed up when I indulged my own curiosity about something or someone and followed my own curiosity down a rabbit hole.

If you're interested in the curiosity back story of these poems, finish reading this now. Or better yet, skip ahead, read the poems, try to guess their back stories, and then come back here to read their back stories. Curiosity doesn't kill readers and poets. These back stories can also be used as writing prompts or activities.

This Stone

This poem happened when I followed the suggestion of my friend Bayo to pick up a nearby object and spend 20 minutes listening to it — far more deeply than I had bothered listening to it before. I chose a large stone on the floor of my bedroom that had been a gift from my friend Martha. Thank you Bayo, Martha, and Cheyenne, the stone.

Together

This poem was inspired by a photograph. I wrote the poem while looking at an amazing image, before I knew what I was looking at. Only later did I learn that it was a close-up photo of a hellbender salamander taken by Joe Milmoe of the U.S. Fish and Wildlife Service. At that point, I added the final stanza to the poem. The photo can be seen on my blog with the poem where it was first published. Biologists and salamanders rule! Thank you Joe.

Welcome to the Void

This poem was inspired by a 4-hour lunch with my friend Knox. He showed up unexpectedly on the island one day, invited me to coffee, and coffee somehow turned into a 4-hour lunch/gab fest/working meeting/therapy session. On my way home, I grew curious about the relationship between friendship, spontaneity, losing track of time, and our amazing ability to create and expand time for friends and loved ones as needed. This poem showed up to teach me more about that. Thank you Knox and curiosity.

When Alien Beings Ask "Why Poetry?" I Offer Them This

I was following two ideas down one rabbit hole in this poem. One: how should I respond when people ask me "Why poetry?" or ask the question I usually get "How could you possibly make a living writing poetry?!" And two: what would it take for my poetry to be read out loud, in public, without me breaking down and crying in the process? Seriously, I'm no public speaker, especially when it comes to reading my poetry. Every time I've been asked to read one of my poems out loud, about half way through, I begin to cry. Not that crying is bad. Tears are an important part of grief and of joy. I'm just curious about what it would take for me to hear my own poetry read out loud without tears. As I followed this curiosity, a new idea showed up: other people reading my poetry instead of me! I began thinking about asking a couple of audience members to stand and read a poem on my behalf: one reading the main lines and another reading stage directions to the other. How fun would that be? Honestly, I'd still probably cry. That's just me. But they'd get through the poem, and we'd likely all have fun in the process, which is what matters to me. Thank you questions and curiosity.

## The Advice of Trees

For 12 years I loved and cultivated the garden and yard at our Seattle home. Then, we moved to Whidbey Island and friends moved into our Seattle home. During a visit back to the Seattle house, I went outside to the back yard to say hello to the trees, my old friends. Happy about my return, the trees decided to impart some tree wisdom to me. Maybe they'd been telling me this all along, I don't know. All I know is that it took me just seconds (and 14 years) to hear it. Thank you trees.

## Our Home is a Poem

One day I noticed that we have gathered a lot of words in our home. Words on rocks. Words on magnets. Words on plates. Words on books. I wondered if I could make a poem using only the words I found around the house. I snapped photos of all the words I could find, arranged the photos, and found a poem. The photos, if you care to see them, can be found in the poem where it first showed up on my blog. Thank you house, objects that speak, and curiosity.

## Jericho Brown Awakens Hearts

I went to a Hedgebrook Winter Salon (look it up: they're so cool) and one of the amazing women there introduced me to the poetry of Jericho Brown, who instantly became my latest poet crush. This just-messing-around, poetic-calisthenics poem is a tribute to Jericho Brown: specifically, his poem Heart Condition. Go find it. Read it. You will not be sorry. Better yet, be a genius and buy one of his books. I get goosebumps just thinking about that poem. Even just reading the title gives me goosebumps. In this tribute poem I play with everything at once, like he does. And I stick closely to the form and playfulness, even the language, of Heart Condition (goosebumps), because I'm a new poet, I'm learning to be as trusting and as honest as he is, and I just needed to hold his hand for a little while. Thank you, master poet, for awakening hearts and poets and courage in your wake.

Sentience (First Draft)

First an experience happened: four deer stepped out onto the road and walked directly toward my car down the middle of the road, causing me to stop the car and look them in the eyes before they moved on. They shifted me outside of the rushed morning commute, outside my spinning mind, and into somewhere else entirely. A feeling arrived: awe at our connection to each other and to everything. Then a question showed up: what will happen when we humans begin thinking about ourselves as one generation instead of 5 different generations? And as one with everything? Then some words began to show up for a poem, but they haven't started to dance yet so this poem isn't done. What happens when you publish an unfinished poem in a book? No idea. Let's find out.

Letting It Be

My friend Bayo was talking about the power of weird actions in pulling forth new writing. Simply doing something weird — for you — for 20 minutes. My poet's heart loved this idea. I immediately went outside on our deck, and instead of sitting on a chair, I sat directly on the deck surface, the gray wood, itself. For 20 minutes. It is amazing what you notice and can see and hear and touch and smell just by shifting slightly outside of normal. Thank you Bayo and my neighborhood.

# This Stone

was a gift from Wyoming
she longed to travel
so a friend pulled her from her field
brought her here to me
to live beside the sea

she found herself in a house of rocks
pulled from every nation
imagined herself at first
in train station

here she was appreciated
not just for her beauty
but for her considerable size and weight
found her calling
holding open a gate

she mentioned that she loves it here
the sea air
friends everywhere
she made just one request

turn me over, she said
you've set me on my face
and I'd like to enjoy the view

mortified
I apologized, though that was not her intent

I lifted her up
we toured the whole place
she met her brethren
sister rocks
met yard and window views
met the cats and dog
all of whom bowed to her, I noticed
when properly introduced

she touched the other gate holder
in our bedroom
her best buddy
face to face

then she sat back down by her gate
to hold it secure against the sea breeze
for Joe the cat
Joey Big Pause, her favorite cat
and I heard her sigh as she took in her view of the sea

or maybe that was me

# Together

distant galaxies
being born
an opening hand
stretching across
the womb of space

touch the darkness
with spinning fingers
new fingertips encountering
creator being created

breathe in the heavy water
here on the sea floor
expel star dust
wiggle new toes

we dance apart
as light within the dark

as dark we soothe
stitching parts
back together

discover within ourselves
hellbender
salamander

# Welcome to the Void

so welcome here
sitting in the sun at a rusty table
lunch with caregivers
in front of Useless Bay
sparrows bathe in dust at our feet
fluff and primp without shame
we admire the audacity

together we swing across Alzheimer's
through marriage troubles
creative projects
travel
waistlines
back into Alzheimer's seamlessly
belly laughs to tears
nuts and bolts to wild imaginings
pain, fear, and giggling back out of ourselves

someone says "I can see when she is leaving
this space-time continuum"

I think "Yes! That's it!"

our grateful multiselves
grateful we don't have to watch
this process from a distance
on the Sci Fi channel
captive to the imagination of strangers

we live this. we who were
born to be space travelers
born to be many
born to weep together publicly
born to swing across space beyond time within selves

content with patchwork ships of friends and duct tape
we have all the time in the world here
I notice now

just home from a 4-hour lunch outside space time self
yet still entirely home
the void, chaos, the space between us,
emptiness herself is home now

I am welcome here.
No, that's not quite it, space travelers.

here, I *am* welcome

so welcome, friends

welcome to the void

# When Alien Beings Ask "Why Poetry?" I Offer Them This

Hello and welcome to earth

[bow with your hands pressed together near your heart.]

[Oh, and if they offer a hand, flipper, tentacle, or anything else to shake, shake it. If they want to hug, hug.]

here in the vastness of space

[throw your arms open wide and look around]

here where seasons and tides are gifts of convention
where time and distance are fluid invention
where music is solace and sunlight is grace

we breathe poetry
we can't help ourselves

[improv a little something to accompany the energy of
words: maybe bounce, dance, spin in a circle, or hum
something]

we can't help ourselves

here we fall in love with a face just because it's a face
here place is a being with exquisite taste
here we fall on our asses laughing

drop to our knees weeping

to remember the feel of soil's warm embrace

here

[indicate the immediate area around yourself, at least:
it's up to you how far your *here* goes]

here

"Why poetry?" makes little sense as a question

poetry is the air we breathe

so our questions tend, instead,
to be variations on this one:

[Shut your eyes and breathe one long breath slowly and
deeply. Then open your eyes and look into their eye, eyes,
or eye equivalents.]

our questions are variations on this one:

How can we breathe more deeply —
right here, right now —
together?

[then shut up, poet]

[shut up and listen]

# The Advice of Trees

be extra kind to yourself, little human
in this interim span
while the world remakes herself for you

you are little for a reason

take solace in walking outside
talking to neighbors
touching the soil and water with your so-cool hands
eating food you made yourself, and that made for you
making love
breathing via those miracle lungs of yours

immerse yourself in some small thing of beauty to you
for you
and when you lose track of time
celebrate this not-small freedom
with a dance of your own making

your dancing feeds our roots, and yours

stop feeling bad for protecting your tender ears
from ongoing media screams
for shading vulnerable eyes from the dark circus politic
for powering down devices
streaming the worst planetary pain

let go of Changing The World
discuss her as a concept endlessly and you can can forget
alternatives

like joining life's dance

can can

on those remarkable feet

can can

like finding your new self fluid

can can

to your surprise and delight

take up one heartfelt project or creature

dwell with it lightly and completely

the difference made there
is felt everywhere

trust us

you connect to life by being you, not by trying to be her

and when you find yourself in the mood to be life herself

in the mood for Changing The World

try shedding your belief in evil

slowly, patiently, as you

can can

little human

That belief keeps distant what life wants closer.

# Our Home is a Poem

You are here
welcome
you rock
grab a beach bucket
an empty journal
or some art supplies

I am at the beach
alone
or chillin with my Gnomies
the birds
or the best husband ever
living the Yoda life
faces turned seaward
beneath a Scooby Doo moon

Guests you are welcome
so be at your ease
help yourselves to some booze
or make yourselves some tea

wabi your sabi alone with a book
or check the tide chart
come join your collective self
down at the beach

# Jericho Brown Awakens Hearts

*A tribute poem to Jedi master poet Jericho Brown. This poem mimics his goosebump-generating, life-changing poem Heart Condition. Go find it. Read it. Buy one of his books. You won't regret it.*

I don't want to hurt a man either, but I like to hear one vacuuming.
Two people touch twice a week, before he leaves for Seattle
On the ferry and again when he comes back to the island.
I don't dare call it long distance, though it feels that way.
I wander the beach alone. Completely. Alone to ponder the fall of
Man, ponder privilege, ponder my shattered family. Content to have
Pain filled conversations with myself the trees and the sea every god
Damn day. Every amazing, blessed day. To solve within myself what I
Cannot solve out there. Alone in our too-snug beach boots, my
Mother, within me, listens to my pain. Quiet. Patient. Curious to
Hear what I work out for myself. My grandmother insists on good
Food and doing all the work herself. I hate to say it, but I am them.
The bad, the good. I shed myself for Mom's Alzheimer's disease.
None of her. I lose none of her. I gain more of her each day. Pull
More of her up and out of me where I can see her. I wish somebody
Had told me we could do that. And while I'm at it, why could no one
Tell me that I'm a poet? Until my new island neighbors showed up
This year, did just that. God gives to each a body. A heart that breaks,
Falls apart. Women live in more than one body. We're all within each
Other's bodies. I wish somebody had told me that too.
When pain mounts in my overworked body, I hurt others. I research
Yoga classes, talk about writing less, exercising more. Buy a wrist
Guard for the failing wrist. Keep writing. Keep talking about doing
Yoga. My vocal cords are smokin' hot right now. In excellent shape
From all the talking about exercise I plan to do. One day soon my
Back pain will drag me kicking and screaming to that class. Or my
Man will. What are you when you leave your man worried about
Your self-inflicted pain? Who leaves their own wrists screaming? Jesus
Christ. I don't want only the weight of our ancestors for us. I want
Their levity yoo. Their weightlessness. Want to float in our collective
Sky, creating. So I grow wings. Become the person who asked for help
And received it. That fabled being who asked for forgiveness:

In asking receives it. Become ok with going on long walks while my Man vacuums. With coming home sweaty. Alive. Ready. Fall into Housework-strengthened arms. My name is Alone and Strong. I come from planet Kick Ass. I am here to learn to love myself as Much as I love you. Here to change our name to Team Jinda, Alzheimer's Improv Troupe #3,051,142.

# Sentience (First Draft)

*blink*

Hello deer who stopped my car with your silent presence
pulled me out of rush hour and into enjoy-this-life day

*wonder*

What if we thought about ourselves as one?
About ourselves as one generation instead of many?

*look*

7 Lessons in Manliness from the Greatest Generation

*listen*

Baby Boomer Generation: The Secrets of Aging
Gracefully

*sniff*

Generation X Is Sick of Your Bullshit

*touch*

Millennials Move Away from Political Party Affiliation

*lick*

Generation Z Brings Tech-Savvy to Whole New Level

*tilt head in silent wonder*


Spokes-Deer for the Flock of Deer

[*welcome friend*]

Sentience

*wow*

[tears]

bow

# Letting It Be

soft paused cat
nose to
velvet bumblebee nose

children down on the beach
yelling to one another
in self-created language:
"Unda buda!" shout lungs
"Oggie buggie buda!" echo other lungs
my brain begins to translate
decides
just let it bee

eyes shift to a new spot
in the far tree
where eagle sits
watching her perfect huge and bumbling brown babies
practice soaring
preparing
for their approaching family vacation

eyes spot my favorite human neighbor
being walked by his timid dog
being led out, up
away from humanity
by a dog who
trembles when
human hands approach her

oh, how I love the invisibility
of sitting on the deck, high up
yet on the deck boards themselves,
on this ground, the gray wood splintering
around me

few human eyes think to look here
won't see outside their own expected
for other humans
so I'm invisible
except to cat
and bird and
bee

except for eagle mama
whose eyes
are always on me
feeling no need to translate

and except for you
sitting
on the sacred
on our asses
on the ground
deciding
together now
just let it be

# Epilogue: Being a Second-Year Poet

This was the year my extended family shattered. The year I begrudgingly became a family elder.

The year I binge-watched all 153 episodes of Gilmore Girls on Netflix because my broken heart needed sappy, beyond-silly TV to help it heal and deal with becoming a voice that is actually listened to.

This was the year I moved with, through, and beyond my own need to hide.

The question Year 2 ultimately asked me was this:

> What does it take to keep creating
> — to keep prioritizing your true self —
> no matter what happens?

The poetry's response:

- Following my artist self and curiosity.
- Strengthening connections within my own poet/writer/artist/ creator
  community.
- Embracing my growing willingness to disconnect from others whenever I need to.
- With the spare time and energy I receive by connecting with creators and by disconnecting with others, as needed, becoming increasingly creative about prioritizing writing no matter what else is happening.

This was the year I recognized how powerful poetry and art actually are. And how connected to other poet and artist and creative selves I actually am.

Together, we saved me this year. Helped me. Healed me. Released me to explore strange new worlds led by little more than my own curiosity.

Poems and artist selves are brave enough to shatter visibly and heal visibly, so our healing properties aren't confined to our individual selves.

Together, we heal the spirit and restore the confidence of the whole world…

Still freaked out. Still lost.
Yet somehow, thanks to you.
We figured out a way to keep doing what we do.
That is the beauty within Year 2.


—Lori, November 15, 2015, Whidbey Island, WA USA

# About the Author

Lori Kane is a poet, writer, coworking space creator, and Alzheimer's care partner. She's serious about home canning and collecting driftwood and stones on beach walks. Aspires to playfulness in all other things. Lori lives on Whidbey Island, Washington, USA with husband and creative partner-in-crime Daniel Gregory, Eva the dog, and Joe, Bella, and Batman the cats.

The poetry and essays in this book reflect the experiences and feelings of being a second-year poet. To find Lori's other books, visit her website at www.collectiveself.com, stop by for a chat on her Lori Kane, Author Facebook page, or follow her @CollectiveSelf on Twitter.

This photo was taken by Daniel. His work can be found at www.danieljgregory.com. He's awesome. Check it out.

# Acknowledgements

Thank you Daniel for continuing to support me through all the ups and downs of being human and being an artist. Best spouse ever.

Thank you Mary "The Canning Monster" for being a great neighbor, friend, and editor. Book #2!

Thank you Bridget for taking the time to read the book, getting to know me better, and for creating stunning book covers! It's so exciting to see the makings of a thoughtful, world-class artist in someone so young. Go girl!

Thank you writers, poets, and artists here on Whidbey, in Seattle, and around the world. You are my lifeblood. And a special shout out to my friends here writing beside me at our new coworking space in the Old Bayview School. You are gifts that never stop healing and replenishing me.

Thank you Jericho Brown for writing a poem that caused me to be far more trusting and vulnerable in writing than I'd ever been before. And thank you, women of Hedgebrook, for introducing me to his work and your own.

Thank you Bayo for putting into words – a lot of words – what I experience and feel. For allowing me to experience through you the value of dark space, of intense and dense writing, not just white space. Allowing me to more fully value my own instincts and self at the very moments I need that the most. What gifts you and Ej and Altheha are – even across vast distances.

Thank you Knox for living a parallel life of community revealing, dementia caregiving, and poetry and for allowing me to witness and learn from you as you juggle it all with humor and honesty.

Thank you family and friends and creatures I encounter in the wilderness for allowing me to write what I write with minimal fear and with an awareness that I'll be supported, loved, and forgiven, as needed.

You are gifts beyond measure.

# Other Books by Lori Kane

*The Grace of Dragons: Receiving the Gifts of Dementia Care Partnering*

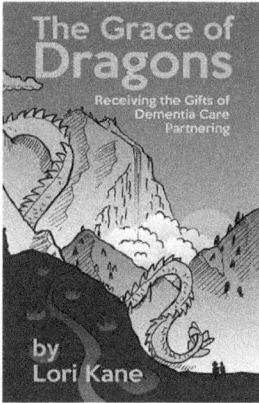

Your poems are…stunning. Reading the poems, it literally felt like something was cutting into and gripping my spirit – emotions caught on a hook. (In a good way – an alive way). You've done it – you have expressed fullness of an experience, in a way that others can enter in. Thank you for sharing! I would love to share these poems with others who lead caregiver support groups.

Marigrace Becker, Program Manager, Community Education and Impact, UW Medicine Memory and Brain Wellness Center

*Reimagination Station: Creating a Game-Changing In-Home Coworking Space*

The book, which was created flash-style in four weeks, is an invaluable tool for home coworking hosts. It's also a rich resource for anyone who wants to grow the connectedness of neighborhoods, create something beautiful and valuable that isn't driven by profit, and extend themselves further into their community.

Cat Johnson, Sharable Magazine

*Year 1 Poet*

Thank you for such wonderful words to remember. My gratitude is endless today because of you.

Sue Reed, a Reader who is not my friend or family member! Huzzah!

*Different Office: Stories from Self-Created, Soul-Satisfying Work Space*

All in all, Different Office, for all its gently humorous and deeply personal explorations of alternative workplaces, is a seminal book. It documents actual, viable alternatives. It takes the idea of work one step further towards fun.

Bernie DeKoven, Game Designer, Author, Lecturer and Fun Theorist

*A Travel Guide for Transitions: Because Freaking Out About This by Myself Totally Sucks*

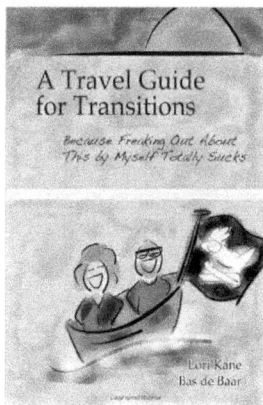

This book has given me the inspiration and ideas on how to be ok with me, the weirdness, the sucky days, and come out ok. I love it – a great read for anyone who feels lost in life or just wants to read about how others are overcoming "normal life" and finding something fantastic by following what they love. The book is packed with whimsical illustrations that really add to the stories and make for a fun easy read.

Tabitha Borchardt, Artist and Avid Reader

*Different Work: Moving from I Should to I Love My Work*

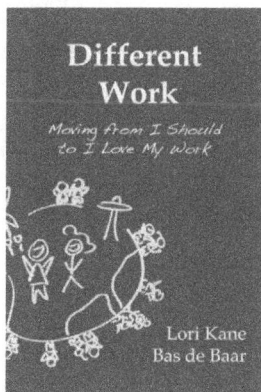

I so related to the Three Amigos story. Their story gave me lots of hope and encouragement to continue the journey. You are an inspiration for folks who are doing the work they love and for those who would like to do the work they love.

Dr. Cathy Fromme, TrustWorks

www.ingramcontent.com/pod-product-compliance
Lightning Source LLC
Chambersburg PA
CBHW031625040426

42452CB00007B/673